Hector Gets Hearing Aids

ADELA VILLALPANDO

GLOBAL
PUBLISHING
SOLUTIONS

1

HECTOR GETS HEARING AIDS by Adela Villalpando

Published by Global Publishing Solutions, LLC
923 Fieldside Drive
Matteson, Illinois 60443
www.globalpublishingsolutions.com

Library of Congress Control Number:
2024942767
International Standard Book Number:
979-8-9900270-5-3
E-book International Standard Book Number:
979-8-9900270-6-0

Acknowledgements

First and foremost, praises and thanks to God for all the blessings he provides for us on a daily basis.

I would like to thank my husband, Manuel, for his support in helping me achieve my dream of writing this second book. Thanks to my adult children, Melinda, Nicolas, Rodolfo, and Victor, who were also very supportive in the process of completing this book. My grandchildren Matthew and Christian also provided feedback on this book.

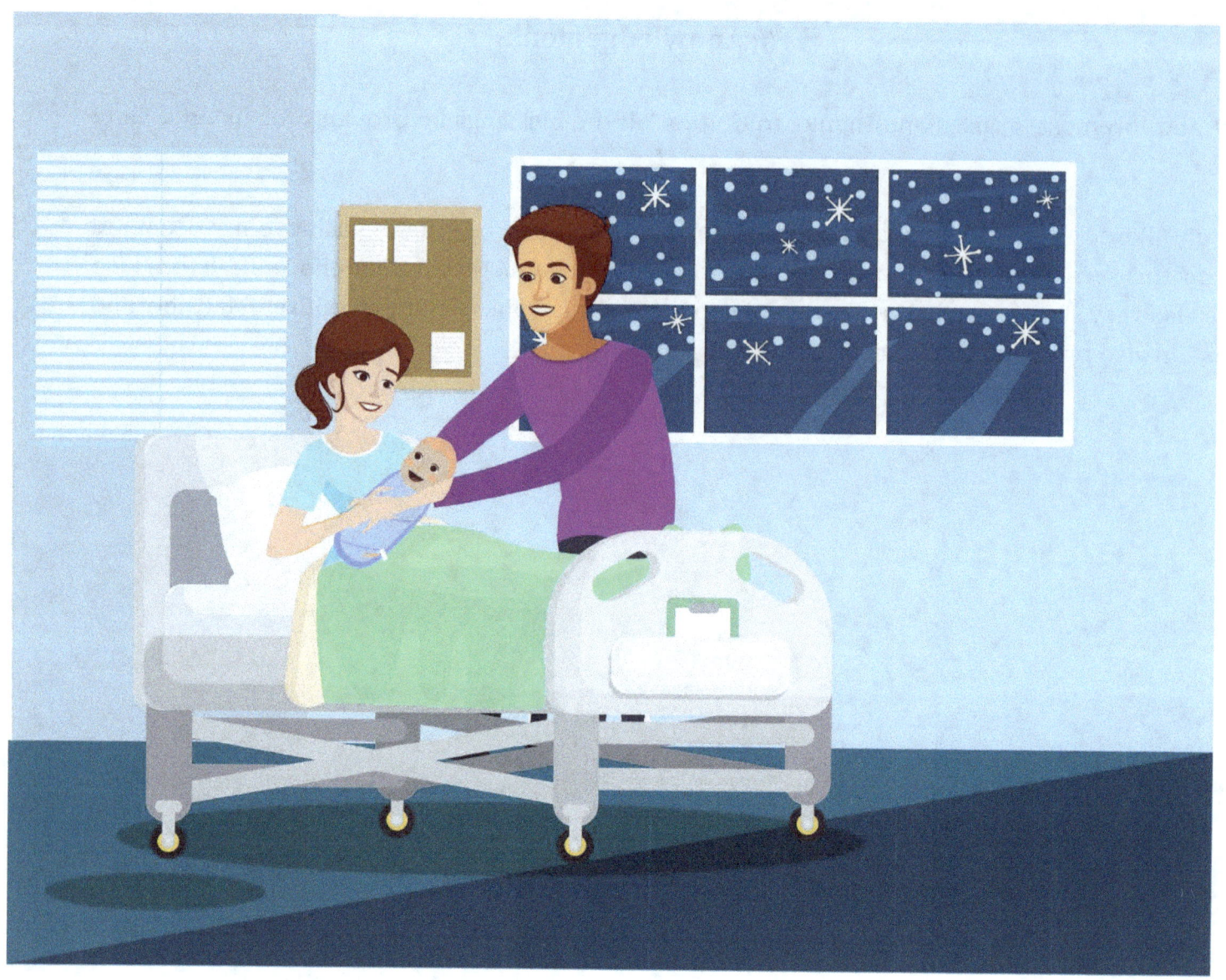

Hector was born on a cold and windy day. His parents were so happy because he was their firstborn. His parents had been wanting a baby for a long time.

Dr. Mark informed Hector's parents that Hector would have to stay in the hospital because he had jaundice. The parents were sad, but it gave them more time to set up the crib and finish decorating his room.

A few days later, his parents got a call from Dr. Mark informing them that Hector was fine. Hector had a series of tests before he was allowed to go home. The parents were nervous but happy to bring him home.

On his first night at home, Hector cried most of the night. His mom did not mind getting up to see what was wrong with him. She was just glad he was home.

There were other nights that Hector just couldn't sleep at night. Hector gained weight and grew as all other babies do.

Hector outgrew his crib, so he got his own bed. He often had trouble going to sleep. Hector would cry because he wanted to sleep with his parents. Mom would read to him until he fell asleep.

His father worked at a grocery store. When he got home, he went straight to where Hector was.

Dad felt that Hector did not hear him because many times he had no facial expression.

There were other times that Dad would cuddle him and whisper in his ear. This gesture made Hector smile from ear to ear.

His mother stayed home and took care of him. She would talk to him and sing to him. She noticed he would giggle when she would sing to him.

On his first birthday, his parents held a huge birthday party for him. Many family members and neighbors came to the party.

Hector was happy but felt uncomfortable with so many people in his house. He did have two friends that Hector liked being with. Jorge and Mario lived nearby, so they often played together.

Ms. Mindy called Hector's parents and explained the situation. Ms. Mindy suggested that they take Hector to get his hearing checked. She said that if Hector didn't hear, he would fall behind academically. He was also beginning to lose complete interest in school and was very unhappy.

Hector's parents were very upset. They did not take Hector to school for three days. Hector was very sad and would cry. He missed being in school. He also missed Matthew, Christian, and especially his teacher.

Since Hector had been present when Ms. Mindy talked to his parents, he knew something was wrong. When he got home, he felt sad, angry, and lonely. He asked his mom if he could get new ears, so he could hear well.

Hector's parents had a talk with Hector. They explained to him that he would need to see his pediatrician and possibly an audiologist. Mom called his pediatrician and explained that she needed an appointment with an audiologist.

So, the appointment was made, and Hector went to his appointment.

Hector was screened, and the audiologist did confirm that Hector would need hearing aids. Mom cried but agreed to order them. She told the audiologist that Hector would wear them.

The next day mom went to talk to Ms. Mindy and share with her what had happened. Mom was afraid that the children would make fun of Hector.

Ms. Mindy assured her that everything would be fine.

Five days after the appointment, Hector went back to get his hearing aids. Once the nurse put them on and adjusted them, Hector said, "Mom, I can hear." Hector's parents were so happy to see Hector smiling but scared of him going back to school.

Hector asked Mom if he could go back to school. Mom agreed that he should go to school. So, the next day Hector was back at school. When Hector walked into the class, all the students cheered, "Yeah, Hector is back!" Matthew and Christian were super excited to have their friend back.

Mom cried, but she was happy to see her son smiling. Hector was happy to be there. Mom left and told Ms. Mindy to please call her if Hector didn't feel like being in class so she could pick him up.

When mom left, Ms. Mindy spoke to the class about how some children and adults need hearing aids in order to hear. Hector quickly touched his hearing aids and said, "Look, I have hearing aids."

Christian said, "Wow, how cool!" Emily said, "They look like small radios." Matthew added, "I am going to tell my mom to get me a pair of hearing aids." "No," said Ms. Mindy unless you need them. She then explained that we all have different needs. For example, some children and adults do need glasses to see.

We also see individuals using a wheelchair because they can't walk.

She continued to talk about hearing aids and how they help individuals that may have a hearing problem.

Matthew said, "Some children have different needs, and that is ok."

Sophie said, "That's a true look at me, I wear glasses." She also added, "My cousin Jenny can't walk, so she has to be in a wheelchair."

The whole class seemed to understand the situation. The children were excited that Hector was in their room once again.

Hector was so glad to be back in class. He a was able to hear everyone talk. He couldn't wait to go home. He wanted to tell his parents how awesome it was to wear hearing aids. Hector kept smiling all day. He felt special since he was the only one that had hearing aids.

All the other children understood that he needed to have hearing aids. Hector finally felt comfortable being part of the class. All throughout the day, Hector kept saying, "This is the best day." He also told Ms. Mindy that he loved school.

The End

Many times, parents are hesitant to get help for their children because they are afraid that other children will laugh at them. Children take care of each other just like adults do. We just need to explain to them the situation, and they will understand what is going on.

It is also important to know that as we get older, we may experience hearing loss and might need to wear hearing aids. If adults do have problems hearing, then they will find it hard to converse with family, friends, or their family doctor. There should be no shame in wearing hearing aids.

Adela and her family working on a farm.

Gilroy, California.

ABOUT THE AUTHOR

Adela Villalpando came from a family of ten. Because she was the second oldest, she had to take care of all of her siblings. That is where her love for caring and nurturing children began.

Adela lives in a small town called Elsa, Texas. This little city is located in the Rio Grande Valley. She has lived there for most of her life. While she was growing up, her family would migrate to California during the summer to work in the fields. A few years later, after her high school graduation, she married her loving husband, Manuel Villalpando.

The couple has been blessed with four children, Melinda, Nicolas, Rodolfo, and Victor. Adela has two grandchildren as well, named Matthew and Christian. The family has tried to make time for each other, and they have created many memories over the years.

Adela has been associated with children throughout her life. She worked for Head Start as a classroom teacher, center manager, disability coordinator, and family coordinator. She was also active in the community and taught bible classes to children for several years. Adela has always been intrigued with children because they are so honest and funny.

She has been teaching pre-K and kindergarten for the past fourteen years at Monte Alto I.S.D.

Monte Alto is a very small community where everyone comes together to help those who are in need of some sort of assistance.

It has been a dream for Adela to be an author, and her dream is becoming a reality with this book. As an educator, she plans to continue writing books. She would like to inspire children and adults that they are capable of fulfilling their dreams if they work hard at it.

Never give up on your dreams.